The

GW01319635

1 The spaceship

'Happy birthday to me. Happy birthday to me,' sang Harry in a loud, cheerful voice. He pushed his hat back onto the back of his head, and sang again. 'Happy birthday dear Harry, Happy birthday to me!'

Police Constable 5601 Harry Evans was driving back to the police station along the country roads of West Yorkshire. He was a short, round man with a friendly face and a cheerful smile. People liked him.

Harry drove through a small village and continued along the quiet country road. He drove round a corner and stopped. There was something in front of him. Something big. Very big. And it wasn't really on the road. It was about one metre above the road. It wasn't doing anything. It was just there . . . a huge, round thing, a thing bigger than a bus, about one metre above the road.

Harry stared. 'What's this? What's happening here?' he thought. 'What is it? It looks . . .' He closed his eyes for a moment. 'Am I dreaming?' he thought. 'Things like this don't happen.' He opened his eyes again. The 'thing' was still there. It was round and silver, wide at the bottom and narrow at the top. The bottom half was

moving round very slowly, and now Harry could see lights in it. Yellow . . . green . . . blue . . . now yellow again. They shone like stars. He watched them. He felt very excited.

Harry turned his engine off and opened the window. It was raining, but there was no sound. No sound at all. No people, no birds, no cars. He turned on his radio. 'PQ to DC,' he said. 'PQ to DC. Come in please.' But the radio did not answer. It did not make a sound.

Harry watched the 'thing' carefully. 'That,' he thought, 'is something very, very strange . . . something from another world, perhaps. It's a spaceship . . . or something like it. I'm going to get out and look at it.'

But Harry did not get out of the car. He couldn't move. Suddenly he felt very afraid. He put his hand over his eyes. 'What's the matter with me?' he thought. 'What's happening to me?' He stared at the spaceship again. It didn't look dangerous. But perhaps it was . . . Harry stayed in the car.

After a few minutes, Harry found his notebook and wrote down the time and place. 'Five fifteen p.m. One kilometre outside Little Ashwell on the Castleford Road.' Then he drew a careful picture of the spaceship. 'But how can I draw the lights?' he thought. He watched them again. They were changing quickly now. Blue, yellow, green, blue, yellow . . . 'They're beautiful,' he thought. 'Like stars.' He wasn't afraid now. He was excited. 'Here I am,' he thought. 'Constable Harry

Evans. I'm not important. Why me? I've seen a spaceship! On my birthday, too! I don't understand it. And who's going to believe me?'

The lights changed faster and faster, and then Harry heard something. 'Somebody's singing,' he thought. No, it wasn't singing, or music. It was just a soft, quiet sound, and it was very beautiful. Harry smiled. He sat quietly, and watched and listened. He felt very happy.

He sat there for about ten minutes. No cars passed, and no people. 'That's strange,' he thought. 'Usually it's a busy road. Where is everybody?'

Suddenly a bright red light shone under the spaceship. Harry put his arm in front of his eyes. The light was too strong. When he looked again, the spaceship was not there. He looked up into the sky and saw a red light. It was moving very fast, much faster than any plane. In two seconds it disappeared.

Harry suddenly felt very tired and very sad. He got out of the car. It wasn't raining now. The road was wet from the rain, but in the middle of the road there was a big dry ring. He walked slowly across it. It was ten metres wide. In the middle there was a small white ring. It was made of white powder. He put some of the powder in a paper bag.

Harry stood up. 'There's a lot of noise now,' he thought. He heard a car, and birds, and the sounds of children. A woman with a baby passed him and smiled. 'Hello,' she said. 'Are you still here?'

'Er . . . yes,' he said. He did not understand her. He was very tired and sad. 'I'm sure it was a spaceship,' he thought. 'It wasn't a dream. It was a wonderful moment in my life. But why me? And why am I so sad now? I don't understand anything.' He got into his car and drove away.

2 Harry's in trouble

Five minutes later Harry arrived at the police station and walked into the building. He passed his friend, Constable Jim Deacon.

'You're in trouble, Harry,' said Jim. 'Where have you been? The Inspector wants you – now!'

Harry hurried to the Inspector's office. 'I mustn't say anything about the spaceship,' he thought. 'Nobody's going to believe me.'

Inspector Barker stood up when Harry came in. He was a big man, with a hard, clever face. He did not smile very often, and he was not smiling now.

'Where have you been, Evans?' he said. 'I wanted you here at half past five. And it's now half past six. Why?'

Half past six! Harry looked at his watch. He was horrified. 'What happened?' he thought. 'It was five fifteen when I saw the spaceship. I've lost an hour!' He looked at the Inspector. 'I'm . . . er . . . sorry, sir,' he said.

'Sorry!' shouted the Inspector. He was angry now.

'That's not good enough, Evans! Why are you late? You went to Castleford about that stolen bicycle. And you left there at five o'clock. It's half an hour's drive from here. *Where have you been?*'

'I . . . er . . . saw something . . . on the road.'

The Inspector sat down and stared at Harry. 'Evans,' he said, 'I'm a busy man. I can't wait all night. *What* did you see on the road? A cat?'

Harry felt unhappy. He never told lies. All his friends knew that. 'What can I say?' he thought. 'It was a spaceship, and I saw it. I'm going to tell him.'

'Well, sir . . .' he began. He told the Inspector everything about the spaceship, and showed him his picture. But he forgot about the powder.

Inspector Barker put his feet on the table in front of him and looked at Harry. 'You saw a spaceship,' he said slowly. 'On the road to Castleford. And did the little men have green faces?' He smiled. It was not a kind smile.

Harry looked hard at the wall above the Inspector's head. 'I didn't see any little men, sir,' he said. 'Or green faces.'

'Evans,' said the Inspector, 'this is a police station, and you're a police officer . . . not a little boy. Go away, and don't tell me a silly story like that again.'

Later Harry saw Jim Deacon again. Jim was a good friend. 'I heard all that, Harry,' he said, 'about the spaceship. I was in the next room.'

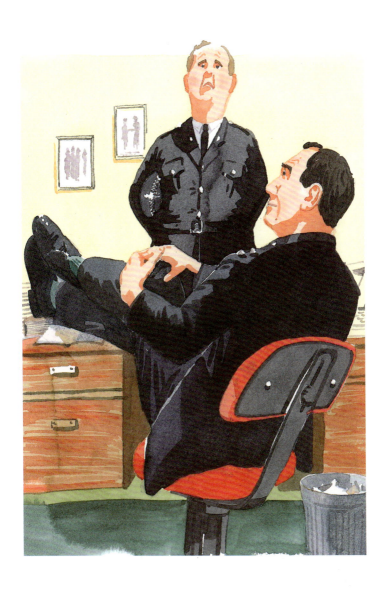

'Barker didn't believe me,' said Harry sadly. 'I'm not surprised. People don't usually see spaceships on the road to Castleford. But I did. Today.'

'Well, I believe you . . . I think,' said Jim. 'Strange things can happen. I haven't forgotten that story about . . .'

'This was different, Jim,' said Harry. 'It was . . .' He stopped. He remembered the lights . . . and the music. No, it wasn't music. What was it? He felt sad again. Then he remembered the powder. 'Look at this, Jim,' he said. He told him about the powder and showed him the paper bag.

Jim was interested. 'Why don't we send this down to the laboratory?' he said. 'We don't have to tell Barker about it. I can take it down there tomorrow.'

'Yes, all right,' said Harry. 'Perhaps the scientists can tell us something about it. Barker has to believe them.'

---

3 A strange story

Jim Deacon knew Harry Evans well, and he liked him. He knew Harry was a good policeman. But it was a very strange story. 'I've heard some strange stories,' he thought. 'But this is the strangest!'

The next day he took the powder to the scientists in the laboratory. Then he drove along the Castleford road to Little Ashwell. He stopped his car one kilometre outside the village, got out, and looked at the road. There was no white powder on the road. Just some old newspapers and a Coke bottle.

'Now what?' thought Jim. He pushed his hat to the back of his head and looked round. Everything looked very ordinary. Birds were singing in the trees. Nothing happened.

Then a woman with a baby came round the corner. She smiled at him. 'Hello,' she said. 'Are you looking for your friend?'

Jim stared at her in surprise. 'Sorry?' he said. 'I don't understand.'

The baby was crying and the woman picked it up. 'You know,' she said. 'The other policeman. The short one. He was here last night. Are you looking for him?'

'Oh . . . er . . . no, not really,' said Jim. 'But . . .'

'Is he all right?'

'All right? Yes, I think so. Why?'

'Well, he looked very strange last night, you know. I thought perhaps he was ill.'

'Did he?' said Jim. 'That's very interesting.' He took out his notebook. 'Tell me about it. What time did you see him?'

'Well, I saw him twice, in fact. I passed him when I was going to the shops at about five fifteen, and then I came back at about . . . er . . . ten past six.'

Jim thought for a moment. 'But . . . what was the policeman doing when you saw him?'

'Well, the first time, when I was going to the shops, he was just sitting in his car. I think he was drawing something. I was very near but he didn't see me. And then, when I got to the end of the road, I looked back. He got out of his car and walked towards the middle of the road. He had his hands out in front of him and a big smile on his face. It was very strange.'

'Yes,' Jim thought. 'That is strange. Harry didn't say anything about that.' He looked at the woman carefully. 'And . . . did you see anything unusual on the road?'

The woman smiled. 'No, nothing.'

'And you didn't hear anything?'

'No. Only the baby. When we left home she was crying, but when we got here she stopped, and began smiling and laughing. She was pointing at something on the road, too. I didn't understand it. I looked, but there was nothing there. Nothing at all. But she was very excited.'

'I see,' said Jim. ('But I don't see,' he thought. 'I don't understand it at all!') 'And then . . . you saw the policeman again, at ten past six? What was he doing then?'

'He was standing in the middle of the road,' answered the woman. 'I spoke to him, but he didn't understand me. He looked sad, and tired. Are you sure he's all right now?'

'Oh yes,' said Jim. 'Yes, yes. He's fine. Well, thank you. You've helped me a lot.'

'That's all right,' said the woman. She walked away. The baby was crying again.

Jim walked up and down for a few minutes, but he didn't see anything. 'What did the baby see?' he thought. 'And why is it crying now? Perhaps it's crying because it can't see the spaceship? Harry was happy when he saw it, and the baby was laughing at the same time. But why didn't the woman see it?'

He thought and thought, but he couldn't find an answer.

4 No one believes Harry

A week later the report on Harry's white powder arrived at the police station. Constable Deacon's name was on the report, but the constable on duty gave it to Inspector Barker. 'This has just come in from the laboratory, sir,' he said.

It was lunchtime and Harry Evans was having a cup of tea upstairs. He was thinking about the spaceship. He thought about it every day. 'I haven't felt happy since that day,' he thought. 'It was a wonderful day. But why did I tell Barker? He didn't believe me. And does Jim really believe me?' He looked sadly out of the window.

Jim found him there. 'Harry,' he said. 'Come on. More trouble. Barker wants us.'

'Oh no. What is it now?'

'That report on the powder. It's just come in, and the fool on duty gave it to Barker,' said Jim.

Inspector Barker was walking up and down his office. He had a piece of paper in his hand. 'Ah, Evans and Deacon,' he said. 'Good. Very good. Perhaps you can help me. I need some help. I don't really understand this. No, I don't. Now . . . listen.'

Harry closed his eyes for a moment. 'I'm not going to like this,' he thought.

The Inspector read from the piece of paper. 'Report number 345834. 14th July. A paper bag with white powder from the Castleford road. When we opened the bag, a lot of strange yellow smoke came out. It smelt very bad. The smoke disappeared very quickly, and there was no powder left in the bag. Perhaps it was interesting, but we cannot make a report. Please send some more of this powder in a glass bottle.'

The Inspector put the report on the table and looked at Harry. 'Is this your spaceship again, Evans?' he asked.

'Yes, sir. I found the powder on the road . . .' He stopped. 'Why, why, why?' he thought. He saw the lights again in his mind, and heard the soft sound of . . . something. What was it? And why?

Jim looked quickly at his friend, and then away again. 'Inspector Barker,' he said. 'I was talking to a woman with a baby near the place. She saw Constable Evans there and she said . . .'

But Barker was not listening to Jim. He was looking at

Harry. 'I'm not interested in spaceships, Evans,' he said, 'or white powders. We're police officers here. We're not playing children's games.'

'I'm not playing games, sir,' said Harry slowly and carefully. 'It was there, and I saw it. I don't understand it, but I saw it.'

'You've been a police officer for . . . how long? Thirty years? That's a long time, Evans,' said the Inspector loudly. 'A long time. Perhaps it's too long. Think about it, Evans. Think about it.'

Soon everybody knew about Harry Evans and his spaceship, and most people laughed at him. 'Have you seen any good spaceships today, Harry?' they asked him. Sometimes Harry laughed with them, but he really felt unhappy and angry about it. And then one day a policeman wrote HARRY'S SPACESHIP on a piece of paper, and put it on Harry's car window. Harry shouted at him, and there was nearly a fight.

Jim met him later in the police restaurant. Harry was sitting alone with a cold cup of tea. He was staring at the wall.

'Why not forget it, Harry old friend?' Jim said. 'It was just a joke – the man thought it was funny, that's all.'

'I don't think it's funny,' said Harry. 'I really saw the spaceship, and it was beautiful, and important, and I can't forget it. I think about it all the time.'

'Yes, I know,' said Jim. Harry's face worried him. It wasn't round and cheerful now – it was thin and sad and

tired. 'But your job's important too, you know.'

'Maybe,' said Harry. 'I don't know.'

'Listen, Harry,' said Jim. 'I've got an idea. You remember the woman with the baby?'

'Yes,' said Harry. 'But that's no good. Perhaps the baby saw it, but babies can't talk, Jim.'

'I know. But the woman can help us with the time problem. She saw you twice. Once at five fifteen and once at ten past six. And she saw you when you got out of the car at five fifteen! You were walking with your hands in front of you. Perhaps you were walking in your sleep!'

'Well, I wasn't!' Harry shouted. 'I wasn't asleep and it wasn't a dream! The spaceship was there! And I didn't get out of the car!'

'Yes, all right, Harry, all right,' said Jim quietly. He was very worried now. 'But there's this problem of time, you see. I think you've forgotten something. Something very important. Listen, why don't you see a doctor? Perhaps . . .'

Harry pushed back his chair and stood up. 'No! Jim, I don't need a doctor! I'm not ill and I haven't forgotten anything! Perhaps you don't believe me, but that's your problem. All right?'

'Yes, Harry. All right,' said Jim softly. 'But . . .'

But Harry was walking out of the restaurant.

Harry Evans did not see a doctor. But he could not forget the spaceship. He thought about it every day. 'It's going to come back,' he thought. 'It's going to come back on my birthday.'

But it didn't come back on his birthday. Harry was very unhappy then. He couldn't sleep for three nights. He had bad dreams. He was very tired and he couldn't eat. Jim Deacon went with him to the police doctor.

-----

5 Harry remembers

Dr Margaret Darcy was an important psychiatrist. She knew a lot about people's thoughts and dreams. She listened to Harry's story, and talked to him quietly and kindly.

'Now, Mr Evans,' she said. 'Would you like to sit in this chair, please? Watch the computer, and listen to me.'

Dr Darcy quietly turned on her cassette recorder. She looked at Jim. 'I always record everything,' she said.

Harry watched the computer. Soft lights shone on and off. Blue . . . green . . . orange . . . pink . . . blue again. 'I like them,' he thought. 'They are nearly as soft as the spaceship lights.' He watched them carefully, and lay back in the chair. He was not asleep, but he was not really awake either.

'Now then, Harry,' said Dr Darcy. 'I'm going to take you back in time. I'm going to take you back to July 8th last year. Your birthday. It's ten past five. Where are you?'

'In my car,' answered Harry slowly. 'I'm driving back

from Castleford.' The room was very quiet. Harry's eyes were closed. 'I can see the spaceship,' he said. 'I'm looking at it. I'm . . . I . . . they want me.' Harry stopped.

'Who want you?' asked the doctor quietly.

'They do,' said Harry. 'I'm getting out of the car. I'm out. It's very quiet. I can see the lights. Blue, yellow, green. They want me. *I'm coming!'*

Harry put his arms out in front of him, while he sat in the chair. 'I'm going towards the spaceship,' he continued. 'There's a door. It's opening. There's a light inside. A beautiful light. All blue, and green – like water. I'm going in. Aaaaah!' He smiled. His voice was very happy. 'I'm inside. I'm in a room – a round room with no doors. I can hear the sound now. It's not really music, but . . . it's very beautiful.'

Suddenly Jim could hear it too. A very quiet, beautiful sound. But it was here, in the doctor's room. He stared at Dr Darcy in surprise, but she didn't look at him.

'Are you alone?' she asked Harry.

'No. There are three of them. They're holding my hands.'

'What are they like?'

'Thin. Shorter than me. They're like thin children with big round heads. They don't have any mouths or noses. Just one big eye. They say . . . they're my friends. They're talking to me! They don't have mouths but I can hear the words in my head.'

'What are they saying?'

18

'LIE DOWN!'

Jim jumped in surprise. Harry's voice was suddenly high and thin like a child's; not a man's voice at all.

'LIE DOWN! WE ARE YOUR FRIENDS. WE MUST UNDERSTAND PEOPLE. WE MUST FIND SOMEONE . . . Hey, I don't like that!' Harry's voice changed again.

'It's a ring,' he said. 'They're putting a metal ring round my head. It's a computer. I don't like it . . . It's . . . it's listening to me. It's making a record of my thoughts. It's . . . aaaaaah! That's better. It's off now. They're looking at it. They're pleased, I think. They . . . YOU ARE OUR FRIEND. YOUR MIND IS OPEN, AND FULL OF LIGHT. IT IS NOT DARK AND CLOSED LIKE OTHER PEOPLE'S MINDS. WE NEED PEOPLE LIKE YOU. WE CAN TEACH YOU. WE CAN SHOW YOU OUR HOME.'

Harry stopped, and a big smile came over his face. Jim could hear the sound very clearly now; a strong, beautiful sound. 'Can you hear that sound, Doctor?' he whispered.

'Sssh! What sound? I can't hear anything,' the doctor whispered back. 'Be quiet.'

Harry looked sad. 'They say I can't go with them. Not this time. They're giving me a drink. I don't want it but I have to drink it. It's very cold! I'm going out of the door. I'm in my car again.'

'Can you see the space people?' asked the doctor. 'Where are they now?'

'What space people?' Harry's voice was angry now. 'I

haven't seen any space people. I have forgotten them. I haven't seen them. Now there's a bright light under the spaceship. I can't look. The spaceship has gone, too.'

Dr Darcy woke Harry up. She turned on the cassette recorder, and they listened to it together. 'How do you feel now, Harry?' she asked.

'I'm not sure,' he answered slowly. 'I'm happy because I saw them again. But why did they leave me? Why didn't they come back?'

'Perhaps they're not real, Harry,' she said quietly. 'Perhaps they're only dreams. Sometimes, when people are very tired . . .'

Harry stared at her in surprise. Then he laughed – a hard, angry laugh. 'Oh, I see,' he said. 'You don't believe me either. The space people are right, then – most people have got closed minds! Come on, Jim. I'm going home. I know I'm not ill.'

---

6 Where's Harry?

A week later, Inspector Barker saw Harry in his office. Barker had Dr Darcy's report in his hand.

'It's no good, Evans,' he said. 'You can't work here now. Police officers don't see spaceships, or little green men with no mouths. I'm sorry for you, but you've lost your job.'

Harry didn't say anything. He just turned round and

walked out of the office. Then he got into his car and drove away.

Very early the next morning Jim Deacon got a call on his car radio. 'DC to RM. Please go to Allerton Lake, north of Little Ashwell. There's an empty car there.'

When he arrived at the lake, Inspector Barker was already there. The empty car was Harry's. Jim stared angrily at Barker. 'What's happened? Where's Harry? Is he dead now, because of you? Because you didn't believe him? Is that it?'

Barker looked unhappy. 'I don't know, Jim,' he said. 'We're looking in the lake. Perhaps his body's in there.'

Jim was very angry. He wanted to hit Barker. He turned and walked quickly away. 'Poor old Harry. Dead because nobody believed him,' he thought.

Then he saw something on the road. A strange ring of white powder. He picked some up in his fingers. But when he touched it, it disappeared in his hand. In a moment there was nothing left.

Jim looked up at the sky, and remembered the strange sound in Dr Darcy's room. 'Is Harry dead?' he thought. 'Perhaps he is . . . and perhaps he isn't. Perhaps he found something last night . . . or perhaps "something" found him. I don't know.'

He looked back at Barker and the empty car. The Inspector was standing by the lake. 'Goodbye, Harry,' said Jim quietly. 'I think you're all right now.'

**Exercises to accompany this story are available on a
photocopiable worksheet in the Storylines Teacher's Guide.**

Oxford University Press,
Walton Street, Oxford OX2 6DP

Oxford   New York
Athens   Auckland   Bangkok   Bombay
Calcutta   Cape Town   Dar es Salaam   Delhi
Florence   Hong Kong   Istanbul   Karachi
Kuala Lumpur   Madras   Madrid   Melbourne
Mexico City   Nairobi   Paris   Singapore
Taipei   Tokyo   Toronto
and associated companies in
Berlin   Ibadan

OXFORD and OXFORD ENGLISH
are trade marks of Oxford University Press

ISBN 0 19 421936 4

Illustrated by Andrew Laws
Design and typesetting by Oxprint Design, Oxford
Series editors: Peter Viney and Bernard Hartley
Printed in Hong Kong